GROUNDING THE CLOUD

Basics and Brokerage

by
Todd D. Lyle, MS

ISBN: 0615972187
ISBN 13: 9780615972183
Library of Congress Control Number: 2014911256
LCCN Imprint Name: Duncan

TABLE OF CONTENTS

Foreword

PREFACE

Grounding the Cloud is designed for you to skip around at your leisure depending on your interest or your cloud services needs.

In addition to the personal narratives herein you will be given directions for establishing your own gateway cloud, assessing your current information technology environment, and for preparing a request for information or proposal from a cloud services brokerage (CSB).

In the following chapters you will have the opportunity to read about how others are profiting from the cloud's utility. These are real people who had problems with their traditional IT infrastructure and found solutions in the cloud by using a CSB.

These individuals are not techies or folks at the help desk trying to impress you with fancy, rapid-fire geek speak. These are business people like you and me. Their stories will help you put a quantifiable meaning to words such as convenience, flexibility, security and risk management as they apply to cloud computing. Their particular needs were different yet their overall objectives were the same. In the end these individuals were able to more effectively problem-solve within their given organizations by applying the benefits of a cloud services brokerage to the process of utilizing cloud services in order to achieve success on a wide array of business goals.

Basic Cloud Hierarchy and Definitions

The following definitions are in order as they first appear in the chapters below.

What is the Cloud?

The Cloud: is an Internet empowered CO-OP of connectivity, data center infrastructures, platforms, processes, middleware and software for the purpose of shared services.

Cloud Models: Public cloud, private cloud and the hybrid cloud - three unique, potentially intermingling types of cloud infrastructures.

Cloud Services Provider (CSP): companies or co-operatives that offer cloud services.

Cloud Services: productivity tools and processes bundled for consumer benefit and utility (e.g. DRaaS, SaaS, PaaS, IaaS and DaaS). Monthly fee or free as opposed to traditional IRS related capitalization.

Cloud Application: a specific productivity tool, also known as an "app".

What is a Cloud Services Brokerage?

Cloud Services Brokerage: (CSB) your cloud middleman, a liaison between technology and business. A CSB lifts the burden of dealing with cloud services providers, vendors and technicians.

Human Element: personalities, expectations and abilities that affect organizations.

Ecosystem: your cloud. The combination of tools and services you use. All of the cloud applications and services you are consuming in your business or personal life from what is available in the cloud.

Cloud Architect: a creator of bundled cloud solutions.

Introduction

Being a child of the Seventies, I grew up listening to music by way of albums played on a record player. Then along came 8-tracks, cassette tapes, and CDs, and before we knew it we were living in an age where we no longer touch our music - it's gone digital. Instead of buying tapes or discs, fans now consume their music by downloading their tunes in the form of MP3 files over the Internet, facilitated by a music middleman to make our listening easier and more efficient.

I'll admit that for me albums provided the more complete experience because of their over-sized artwork. There was the tactile fulfillment offered by physical ownership. The bottom line is advancements in technology have made owning, protecting, and accessing our favorite music a lot easier. Of course there are those who will debate whether or not music sounded better on vinyl, but in a time where we can literally hold 20,000 songs in the palm of one hand, the convenience and utility offered by digital music is simply unquestionable.

Rapid developments in technology have benefited the world of business just as much as the consumer. In business, arguably one of the single biggest advancements over the last twenty years has been the advent of cloud computing. Today this allows us to have instant access to our data without the need for owning expensive, bulky, physical servers.

In the final analysis, I suggest that records, tapes, and CDs are to MP3's what on-site servers are to cloud computing. Here is the takeaway and the reason I wrote this book: I believe a cloud services brokerage (CSB) is to your business what iTunes is to your music - a very useful middleman that will make your business interactions in the cloud simpler and more efficient. My goal is for you to come away with an appreciation of cloud-based technologies, their potential in our everyday business lives, and the benefits of organizing your interaction within the cloud through a cloud services brokerage.

Tech Stuff

What is the Cloud?

It seems that the cloud is stuck being thought of as merely online backup. It is more than that. The cloud is an Internet empowered CO-OP of connectivity, data center infrastructures, platforms, processes, middleware and software for the purpose of shared services. These services and processes grant you, the manipulator of the keyboard or device, the ability to exchange the data necessary to accomplish your goals and tasks.

When you upload a video to YouTube, you are allowing it to be stored on one of a million or so (Google doesn't share the exact number) public servers operated by Google. When you post pictures on Facebook you are uploading your data to one of the hundreds of thousands of servers owned and operated by Facebook.

In each of these situations you are utilizing the power of the cloud. This power is being generated by cloud services providers (CSP) who are serving millions of users at any given time.

When computing through the cloud you pay for what you consume. When you purchase physical software you own it whether you use it or not. This can create scenarios for wasted resources. There is no tangible product with the utility of the cloud. Because of this, you are only paying for what you use – just like you only pay for electricity when you have the lights on.

On-demand video giant Netflix has chosen to use Amazon Web Service's (AWS) data centers and other public cloud offerings to meet their business goals of storing and streaming their content to you. This is something you receive as a service, not a product.

The public cloud that Netflix uses is one of three unique, potentially intermingling types of cloud infrastructures. The three infrastructures are public cloud, private cloud and the hybrid cloud. The preference is often up to you and your business needs. On the flip side, your business needs may drive a hybrid scenario when your line of business application becomes a legacy system or there are no public cloud solutions to meet your needs.

The manner in which forces combine to provide movies via Netflix is an example of why the public cloud is my first choice of cloud infrastructures. It represents the gold standard for commoditized utility computing.

With the public cloud model the software productivity tools to which you have become accustom do not run on hardware in your office. You will be working on rented virtual or physical server(s) through an application program interface (API) that allows you to peer into your productivity tools from the device of your choice.

Public cloud services providers such as Amazon Web Services (AWS), Dell, and Rackspace offer resources such as storage and an array of applications available to you over the Internet. These offerings may be free or on a pay-per-use schedule.

While I am a champion of the public cloud model, I appreciate the state of our world economy and recognize that most of us don't have the time, money or additional leadership necessary to make what may appear to be an all-or-nothing change in our information technology infrastructure. Therefore, you can wait until your present systems require replacing or begin breaking down. At that point you can avoid capitalizing these expenditures by embracing the public cloud.

The private cloud is the second of the three cloud options. Unlike the public cloud, the private cloud infrastructure is operated solely for your organization and is owned and maintained by you. This is at your capital expense, though all of your data moves over the same public telecommunications systems as the rest of us. Usually, the private cloud or server(s), as you may be more familiar with calling them, are located off-site at a data center. Even though your infrastructure is off-site it still requires a significant degree of engagement by you. Servers, software, and licenses all need to be purchased and maintained and eventually re-purchased. Cloud service providers such as GoDaddy, 1&1, and Rackspace offer private cloud options as do many local data centers.

These companies will install your system, maintain it, and act as your managed services provider.

There are some who argue a private cloud can also be defined as the traditional model of physically having the hardware on-site with employees logging in through a virtual private network (VPN), terminal server, or other Internet-based portal. Currently, many business owners use one of these types of access so their employees are able to share data within their company domain. This all may seem like semantics, but it is more than that. If you are capitalizing the expense, you are expending resources that might be better applied elsewhere in your business.

To overcome some of the challenges presented by a purely public or private cloud there is a third infrastructure available: the hybrid cloud. This is a composition of utilizing public cloud offerings, such as Email and off-site backup, while continuing to use your on-site or private cloud-based productivity resources. All of your unique tools can be bound together with public infrastructure offering you the benefits of a multiple deployment model.

There are a couple of immediate reasons why the hybrid model may be ideal for you. First, the reason I find the hybrid cloud to be a practical option is because a viable public cloud solution is not always available. Unique customer relationship management software (CRM) or enterprise resource management software (ERP) may not be profitable enough for development into a software as a service (SaaS) offering. Usually, this is due to a particular software serving too small a market for its developers to invest in making it into a cloud based service. Therefore, particular niche software will need to continue to run on your current environment. However, this doesn't mean you shouldn't run your other IT requirements through the public cloud; you should, but you will be running in a hybrid environment.

The second reason for the hybrid cloud is to provide for an organization's capacity planning and rapid deployment requirements. Utilization of a hybrid cloud in this manner is known as cloud bursting. Cloud bursting allows for scaling across infrastructures. Basically, when you run out of room on your original configuration you can take up tenancy on the public cloud. When demand recedes you can go back to your original configuration. The advantage of cloud bursting is that an organization will only pay for what it uses.

There are operational, legal, and risk management reasons that demand some businesses to perpetually run in a hybrid cloud environment. For the rest of us there are cloud services providers who offer an array of services and API's. Cloud services can best be described as hardware and middleware and software that does something on your behalf with limited input from your perspective. Since, in most cases, services are metered, you are able to control resources and use as little or as much of the service(s) you need.

Confounding as the cloud may seem, its lexicon is even more so, the following will help you gain an appreciation for DRaaS, SaaS, PaaS, IaaS and DaaS.

DRaaS or disaster recovery as a service provides comprehensive risk mitigation coverage. Your whole operation can be continuously replicated and your daily operational tempo rapidly recovered, perhaps without interruption, in the event of a catastrophic incident. DraaS can be the contingency plan for your entire organization.

Recognizing that disaster recovery (DR) is the underpinning of your continuance, DR should be integrated into everything so that you can rapidly restart your business.

Most commonly offered via Apple, Google or Microsoft app stores is **SaaS** or software as a service. SaaS is a delivery model in which the productivity software and all of the associated workflow are hosted in the cloud. There are many different SaaS available to you and they do almost anything you can imagine. Some SaaS you may be familiar with are Google Docs, iWork and Microsoft 365. The majority of SaaS are accessed via a web browser on the device of your choice. Almost every enterprise software vendor has incorporated SaaS into their offerings. There are many advantages to adding SaaS to your business strategy. One of its biggest selling points for companies that have already adopted it is the potential to reduce information technology support costs by outsourcing related matters to a SaaS provider. As this is written, spending on SaaS is outpacing spending on on-site enterprise applications.

PaaS or platform as a service is another cloud service category. In this model, the service provider offers the networks, servers, storage and other services that are required to host your software and applications. The offerings of PaaS allow for the deployment of your proprietary business software application without the cost and complexity of maintaining and managing the hardware and software that goes along with it. Most PaaS providers allow you to create a server environment by building processes that meet your needs from a set of templates provided by the cloud services provider(s) of your choice.

Shoulder-to-shoulder with SaaS and PaaS is **IaaS** or infrastructure as a service. IaaS providers offer it all; they are able to meet almost every consumer need. They provide computers, physical as well as virtual machines, and they offer related consulting resources. These are the companies with data centers all over the world: Dell, Hewlett Packard, Microsoft, Amazon, Google and Rackspace. They support a large number of physical and virtual machines and have the ability to rapidly scale services up or down according to requirements. IaaS providers offer you additional services and resources such as firewalls, load balancers, software bundles, virtual local area networks (VLANs), file-based storage, virtual-machine disk image library, and even your own Internet protocol (IP) address.

Those of us who grew up with a Windows Desktop have grown accustomed to its look and feel. We enjoy being able to access the same configuration every time. It is comfortable. Fortunately as bandwidth and processing power continue to increase so does the option for cloud-based desktops. Desktop as a Service or **DaaS** allows you to peer into the very same desktop every time from any device.

Once an understanding of the cloud sets in, many people become concerned about security, questioning the safety of their data once it becomes part of the "public realm." Legal, governance, risk management, and compliance all play a role in our lives and some organizations such as financial institutions, law firms, and hospitals feel they can't use the public cloud.

We have all heard the controversy of the United States National Security Agency (NSA) sneaking into our lives, especially when it comes to our activities online. It is true; being on the Internet whether through the public cloud or a private server makes you more susceptible to prying eyes. However, with the resources provided by various reputable organizations the public cloud is among the safest places to store your data.

Current estimates by Gartner indicate that $156 billion will be spent on public cloud services in 2014. The cloud is no longer a fringe strategy. It is mainstream, with the hybrid model becoming the preferred method of consumption for most businesses.

Points of Interest:

1. The cloud is an Internet empowered CO-OP of connectivity, data center infrastructures, platforms, processes, middleware and software for the purpose of shared services.
2. There are three types of cloud infrastructures: public cloud, private cloud, and hybrid cloud.
3. Cloud services can best be described as a productivity tool that does something on your behalf without your knowing how it was done. You are able to use as little or as much of this service as you need.
4. There are several different types of services offered through the cloud. The best-known services are: DraaS, SaaS, PaaS, IaaS and DaaS.
5. With the resources provided by reputable cloud organizations, the cloud is about the safest place to store your data.

What is a Cloud Services Brokerage?

Daryl C. Plummer, Vice President & Fellow at the well-known and respected information technology research and advisory firm Gartner, is credited with coining the term cloud services brokerage (CSB) and developing the concept in the market place. He states that, "(a) CSB is what gets the consumer out of the 'between a rock and a hard place' problem of not having to become an expert in the details of how a cloud service is delivered." (Forbes Magazine, March 22, 2012).

Gartner, the first analyst firm to begin actively writing on the subject, suggests that CSB's should have a division of expertise. They take the position that a brokerage should be defined in terms of the services that may be expected from a CSB. Gartner categorizes four main services: aggregation, integration, governance, and customization.

Forrester Research, another analyst firm, takes the position that a CSB should specialize in specific expertise in order to provide the best business service(s). Forrester has divided proficiencies into three categories: simple cloud broker, full infrastructure broker, and SaaS broker. In addition to worldwide organizations such as Gartner and Forrester there are many individual experts in the field that have their own opinions.

IT analysis, market research, and consulting firm Interarbor Solutions LLC's Principal Analyst Dana Gardner asks readers to *"envision some kind of cloud middleman, helping to cut through the plethora of cloud options and services."*

In addition to these and other analyst firms there are many bloggers who are plying the market place with their own CSB definitions. Bloggers such as Margaret (Peggy) Rouse (TechTarget.com) describes a cloud services brokerage as, "(a) cloud broker is a third-party individual or business that acts as an intermediary between the purchaser of a cloud computing service and the sellers of that service. In general, a broker is someone who acts as an intermediary between two or more parties during negotiations."

Editor-in-chief of Techopedia, Cory Janssen explains that, "(a) cloud broker generally works on typical brokerage process principles. They assist cloud buyers with decision making by helping them evaluate, shortlist, and select a cloud vendor or solution based on specific requirements."

Clearly there are many opinions on the definition of a cloud services brokerage. In all, there is a common theme - a CSB is a middleman, a liaison between technology and business.

It is important to understand the difference between internal and external cloud services brokerages. Currently most CSB are external, meaning that they work outside of your business; they are like a Real Estate Broker or Insurance Agent - a third party that you may engage. There is also the internal CSB. You are just beginning to find these in public sector (government) agencies and very large businesses.

When it comes to the external CSB, the three types of cloud service brokers Forrester differentiates between are: simple cloud broker, full infrastructure broker and SaaS broker. The simple cloud broker is able to provide a mass of knowledge and help within one cloud segment, either Infrastructure (IaaS) or Platform (PaaS) services. The full infrastructure broker is able to provide service across public, private, and hybrid clouds and can offer a wide range of services. A software (SaaS) broker researches SaaS providers and is able to offer presale suggestions and after-the-sale services such as unified billing, service level agreement monitoring, and contract management. Forrester foresees a single company might deliver more than one type of cloud brokerage model.

Gartner believes that there are four areas of expertise. Gartner's list includes: <u>Aggregator</u>: a broker that bundles cloud services and offers them to clients. <u>Integrator</u>: brokers that are highly technical and who merge (bundle) services from a variety of cloud providers to create a net-new business product. <u>Governor</u>: brokers that ensure that the cloud provider chosen is appropriate and has the ability to treat the data in accordance with regulations and practices for specific country and industry guidelines. And lastly, the Customizer: brokers that create extensions to existing cloud services to perform a specific task and then ensure that the extensions work correctly.

"As [consumers] move to the cloud, they will need help to determine which options are right for them — and then put them all together." (*Lauren Gibbons Paul, channelprosmd.com, February 09, 2012*).

While each definition discussed here exhibits similar characteristics, each has its own take on the responsibilities and approach to providing brokerage services. I believe that the analysts, experts, and the lack of standardization have contributed to the relatively slow embrace of the cloud's full potential.

In addition to valuing their expertise, you must find a level of trust with your CSB and its representatives as you would any other member of your business team. Your CSB should work hand in hand with you and learn all of your specific needs with respect to your business requirements. They should advise you of performance, costs, security, risks, and standards unique to your business and industry. A CSB should be up to date on all regulations, privacy issues and case law that may impact your business.

Considering our reliance on information technology it is surprising that most companies do not have their business resources aligned to address their IT dependence. Roughly a quarter of the world's workplaces report that they do not have enough finances or staff to keep pace with their in-house IT requirements.

Dropping down another layer in the world of cloud services brokerages, you will find brokerages that specialize in managing the human element of technology – also known as the soft side of IT. This is something very few experts discuss. However, it is something every business has to deal with no matter the industry, size, or specific IT requirements. Dealing with the human element is the core strength of a specialist cloud services brokerage (SCSB).

A SCSB has a fiduciary responsibility to their consumer, and in today's economic environment they should recognize the lack of resources available to most of us. They should work with you to design a cloud strategy that addresses the lifecycle of your current hardware and software and its support. (e.g., Microsoft's April 2014 goal for no longer supporting Windows XP, their most popular operating system of all time.)

In cases like Microsoft's legacy action of retiring XP support, your CSB should be proactive in addressing your business-essential systems before your systems run out of warranty or support. They will assist with procuring cloud-based solutions that ease your capital outlay and demand on the human element.

A specialist cloud services brokerage should coordinate all aspects of your IT ecosystem by providing cloud-scale provisioning, unified management and unified billing, service level agreement management, and accessible customer support.

A SCSB will lift the burden of dealing with cloud services providers, vendors, and technicians. With a SCSB you have someone middle-manning the situation, proactively addressing your specific business needs so that you don't find yourself holding a help ticket or waiting on an Email response.

Picture Ben Franklin attempting to harness electricity from a lightning-filled sky. The key tied to his kite was the middleman between electricity and the ground. Similarly, a specialist cloud services brokerage can be the key to your business finding success in the cloud. The SCSB exists to help businesses consume cloud solutions by adding value, reducing risk, and increasing your understanding of the cloud while enhancing the services delivered.

Once you have established that you are ready to take the first steps to the cloud and decide you are going to use some assistance in getting there, you need to be prepared. You should consider the goals you want to achieve prior to hiring a SCSB or any other consultant for that matter. I have provided a list of questions at the back of this book that can help you determine your objectives and thus will aid you in finding the best SCSB to assist in creating your ecosystem.

A specialist cloud services brokerage should be an expert in analyzing your business and working with you to identify what cloud solutions will best meet your requirements. Another added value of an SCSB is that its cloud architects continuously search for and scour cloud options. They play with the hardware, middleware, and software so that the SCSB can bring you the best solutions at utility pricing. Think of a SCSB as one part Underwriters Laboratories as they certify, validate, test, inspect, audit, advise and train and one part Butler as they provide attention and ongoing care. Once your SCSB has heard your goals and worked with you to select the appropriate providers they will bundle your services for ease of consumption.

A specialist cloud services brokerage can help you put together your cloud strategy with consideration to continuity planning and risk management. Moreover, your SCSB will remain vigilant in monitoring your metered cloud services. Your SCSB is there to ensure that when an employee leaves your organization, you can quickly lock them out or down and stop paying for that individual's related usage. This kind of oversight provides the continuity and stability that is required to keep your ecosystem in step with the daily happenings of your business. The SCSB is your concierge to the cloud.

A reputable SCSB does not receive compensation from any of the cloud service providers, companies, or consultants they present. There should not be a conflict of interest between the SCSB and the companies it is managing for you. A SCSB should be working for you and for the betterment of our collective utility.

With the landscape of technology constantly changing, you should not have to expend your energy keeping up. By delegating a corresponding level of responsibility to a SCSB, you will benefit from their operational knowledge and experience in governance, risk management, and return on investment.

The potential of the cloud services brokerage model has caught the attention of the U.S. Government. In March 2014, The Government Services Administration (GSA) completed a pilot program where they analyzed ways of changing user behavior to maximize the US government's concept of shared services. Their findings are currently driving policy based on the retail sector's category management concept thus leading them towards the preparation of what they are calling a Common Acquisition Platform (CAP).

A number of government organizations offer their own model and opinion on the topic of the cloud and the CSB. One of the leading organizations on the topic is the National Institute of Science and Technology (NIST). NIST states that a CSB needs to provide aggregation, arbitrage, and intermediation. There are other internal CSB's emerging within the National Nuclear Security Administration (NNSA) and the United States Department of Energy (DOE) however, government agencies are challenged because they are encumbered by regulations and a lack of education.

Whatever your position, organization or need, a cloud services brokerage can assist you in your move to the cloud. You won't be alone in your decision to use a CSB. Gartner estimates that the cloud services brokerage will become the single largest cloud service consumed by 2015. According to Gartner, "By 2015, at least 20% of all cloud services will be consumed via internal or external cloud services brokerages."

Points of Interest:

1. With a CSB, you have someone middle-manning the situation, proactively addressing matters so that you don't find yourself holding a help ticket or an Email waiting for a response.
2. You should be able trust a CSB and its representatives as you would any other member of your business team as they are more than just part of your IT solution.
3. A SCSB will handle the soft issues of technology because there is more to technology than just understanding the hardware and the software.
4. There are several different definitions, explanations and opinions of what a CSB is, how it should operate, and what it should provide.
5. A SCSB can assist you in the set up and management of both the technical and business aspects of your cloud.

What is the Human Element?

The cloud. Cloud storage. Cloud computing. Cloud services. The amount of words "they" have attached to the cloud can make your head spin. But don't worry, it is also making their heads' spin as well. Until there is baseline knowledge with basic definitions, adoption of cloud services will be slow.

It is no wonder there are general stereotypes that the cloud is nothing more than off-site backup or a glorified storage center for your files, photos, and music. These stereotypes tend to touch on the simplicities of the cloud but they are missing out on the nuances and the depth of the cloud.

My goal is to make the cloud understandable so we can all take advantage of its benefits. First, yes, the cloud is a wonderful option for file sharing, backing-up your data, Email, et cetera, but it allows for so much more. The cloud and its service providers offer a multitude of cost-efficient solutions that you may not be aware of, or may not be empowered to incorporate in your decision-making process. In the world of business (private sector) the need for short-term profits often drives decisions and alliances. Your colleagues and employees are not always open to sharing new ideas or methods for success. Government agencies (public sector) are often controlled by outdated policies or purchasing procedures. Current standard operating procedures make timely acquisition of off-the-shelf solutions problematic. These daily operational or administrative problems, in addition to cultural and environmental challenges, play on the human element.

In our private lives, new devices and applications are available through marketplaces such as Apple, Microsoft, and Google. You probably use several applications and services in your personal life such as online banking, tax preparation, or electronic books and newspapers. At home we have more easily adapted to cloud-based technologies, however many of us are still fearful of exposing our sacred business data to that very same cloud. We can't let fear hinder us from innovation and business productivity.

Taking a logical and methodical approach will help allay your fears in preparing a cloud strategy. Just as you decided what applications and services were right for your personal life, you can do the same in your business life when properly empowered. It starts with education and the resultant comfort of knowing your data is and will be secure. You will be relieved once shielded from the complexity of operating and maintaining your capitalized software and hardware.

To affect change and achieve success, consideration must be given to the personas, expectations, and abilities of your current and future users. The proper education of your organization, from management to end-user, is as essential to your success as is selecting the right combination of cloud services providers (CSP). Simply stated: empower your people, as they are the soft side of information technology (IT) and much more fluid.

It is not just the purpose, function, and efficiency of the application or service you need to consider. You must also give thought to the end user's learning curve and the man-hours spent on transition activities as opposed to actual productivity. Analyzing your core needs will help lead to *your* best choice and, often, your business needs can be achieved with the public cloud.

When it comes to migrating to the cloud, service providers such as Rackspace have been able to hide many of the issues of conversion from a desktop application to a cloud-based application by keeping a similar look to the interface, thereby limiting your employee transition time. When a change occurs, most Rackspace users do not even notice they are consuming a new product.

Beyond the mobility of your productivity tools the use of cloud services can lead to the elimination of all of your in-house servers. As a businessman, I think that this is one of the biggest benefits the cloud brings to any organization.

Nothing bogs you, your IT staff, or consultants down more than the mundane tasks of running back-ups, providing hardware maintenance and updates, and installing patches on your server(s).

In addition to this ongoing operational hassle and expense, your servers should be replaced about every three years. The cost per server hardware is often between $6,000 and $8,000 [2013 US dollars] for a basic configuration. In addition, there are the licensing fees, software costs, tech-service consultant fees, and all of the other financial and risk management obligations involved with owning your own infrastructure. The cloud helps lift the burden of disaster recovery, hardware and software meltdown, security, and governance off of your shoulders while minimizing or eliminating expenses related to the same.

It is not easy to turn over the life force of your business to a service provider with whom you have not done business. This is a normal feeling. It is also normal to want to touch whatever it is we are paying for, even though we may not fully understand what is "in the box" (the server). This emotion is what private cloud marketing activities exploit, because most people fear letting their business data off premise. It can feel like you are leaving your baby at a new daycare and hoping that the provider will keep your child safe and tend to their unique needs. Resistance to change is what makes it hard to change from what you think is working to what will possibly work better.

Cloud services are resilient and are built with expansion and contraction in mind. Cloud services are coming at us fast. For now, it is up to you to decide whether to consume the cloud as a utility. The public cloud is rented, not owned. Preparation need not be daunting. With the help of a cloud services brokerage you can take charge of related budgets, governance, processes, and protocols.

The cloud services brokerage model is designed to get between you and the sometimes disconnected and seemingly disinterested cloud services providers. A CSB is there as your middleman and can be operated internally or externally by a third-party. To address the human element and our avoidance to change the specialist cloud services brokerage (SCSB) was conceived.

A specialist cloud services brokerage will hold your hand throughout your cloud journey. A SCSB provides unified management and billing via one monthly invoice covering many cloud services. As a one-stop shop, a SCSB combines consulting, system integration, and outsourcing capabilities with cloud services bundles. A SCSB designs, implements, and manages cloud-first solutions. According to the information technology research and advisory firm Gartner, specialist cloud services brokers play an important role in addressing the human element helping you with <u>GROUNDING THE CLOUD</u>.

Points of Interest:

1. *Human Element:* personalities, expectations, and abilities that affect organizations.
2. While people are likely to embrace new technology in their personal lives, they are hesitant to do it when it comes to their work environment.
3. The specialist cloud services brokerage (SCSB) was designed to address the human element and the avoidance of change.
4. A SCSB should be an expert in analyzing your business and working with you to identify what cloud solutions will best meet your requirements.
5. A SCSB can help you put together your cloud strategy with consideration to continuity planning and risk management.

Real World

Duncan, LLC

On November 23, 2011, we dismantled our server room. I felt relief as the big Dell coffin was wheeled out along with its seven servers and what seemed to be about 400 miles of cables. As the truck pulled away I felt calm and a sense of satisfaction. It was as if the weight of the world had been lifted off my shoulders knowing that from this day forward my data would be safe and secure and that I was no longer responsible for the daily grind of caring for my on-site IT infrastructure.

Since August 2007, I had been planning, implementing, experiencing setbacks, and ultimately growing as a specialist cloud services brokerage (SCSB). My vision of relying on an all-public cloud ecosystem was for Duncan, LLC to be like Underwriters Laboratories Inc., constantly testing new cloud tools and advising on the most appropriate productivity tools for the time.

Today, every single technical operation of my business is conducted in the cloud. With the assistance of cloud services architects, business risk managers, and industry analysts, I vetted numerous cloud services providers and selected several that you will read about in this chapter. Concurrently, I established relationships with a full spectrum of system engineers and process consultants who can thoroughly speak to their services and the burgeoning cloud culture.

I chose to build an all-cloud company to demonstrate the utility potential similarly experienced with reputable electric and water utilities. Sorting through the breadth of options and then forcing my reliance on them was intended to enforce trust in the cloud model and provide ongoing peace of mind for all involved.

Beyond the day-to-day operational benefits, the overall advantage of the public cloud is risk management. From a practical perspective, I have developed a cost efficient business productivity platform for conducting commerce starting with: no credit card machines, no paper invoices or unchecked quality issues created by us, the human element of technology.

Designed for constant change, Duncan, LLC emerged from a traditional IT infrastructure to a scalable all-cloud model.

Since my goal was to create a company based on utility computing, it is fitting to begin with two of today's largest cloud services providers. I happen to utilize both of them in my cloud bundles: Amazon Web Services (AWS) and Rackspace.

Amazon Web Services (AWS) is a collection of remote computing services that together comprise a cloud computing platform. AWS offers almost any infrastructure (IaaS) and platform (PaaS) you could want. Currently they are not end-user oriented. Rackspace however is customer centric offering "the Fanatical Support promise".

According to a March 2013 report, DataCenterKnowledge.com estimates that Rackspace has well over 94,000 servers in operation with Rackspace's virtual machines being powered by OpenStack - the world's leading open-source cloud operating system. Like many cloud infrastructures, they can quickly scale for usage. Rackspace allows you to manage the deployment, specifications and performance of the servers yourself or Rackspace offers the services of its internal cloud services brokerage at a premium to manage your cloud usage and service levels.

While the two major players in the world of IaaS and PaaS sound similar in theory and both companies are offering similar services, they are fundamentally different companies. From start to finish their business plans couldn't be further apart. Rackspace is geared toward the end-user. This is not the case with Amazon Web Services (AWS). AWS is focused primarily on their services yet they do offer comprehensive online setup for those who are familiar with IaaS and PaaS.

Amazon Web Services continually adds new products. Its two main web services are Amazon EC2 and Amazon S3. Amazon EC2, or Amazon Elastic Compute Cloud, is Amazon's public cloud and is also their PaaS. In 2010, Amazon began hosting Amazon.com on Amazon EC2.

Amazon S3 or Simple Storage Service is an online file storage web service. This is simply storage. In April of 2013, Amazon reported that over three trillion items were stored on Amazon S3. Among its other offerings is AWS Marketplace where you can purchase pre-selected software; they offer both licensed software and SaaS options. Choosing software is an automated process done over the web. You are responsible for managing all of your software choices and server usage via a dashboard otherwise known as an API.

Besides AWS and Rackspace there are other big names in the IaaS and PaaS arena. GoDaddy is available for individuals with smaller scale needs. They offer a private cloud, Email services, domain name reservations, and web hosting and design services. GoDaddy is an Internet Services Provider (ISP), therefore they do not offer the public cloud and many of the other assets to make them a suitable choice for most businesses.

Google offers cloud solutions and a large selection of APIs. Its offerings are very much geared towards developers and while they are super cool, they are not necessarily what the non-technical person will understand. Google has a free public cloud offering that is more user friendly, however one drawback to free is they scan your data for analysis and marketing endeavors. In other words, Google reads, uses, and sells your stuff. It is not just Google that scans your data. All too often when you use free services the providers scan your communications and build user profiles that they then sell to third parties. This is how you receive those very personalized advertisements.

In March 2014, Google launched a variety of updates to its cloud platform designed to increase competition by addressing Amazon's position in the marketplace. Google drastically reduced their prices. That further drove the public cloud initiative and set a precedent for their model of cloud services. It also brought down the overall price of cloud services. Google also launched its BigQuery Streaming. This new platform ingests over 100,000 rows of data per second, making this information available for real-time analysis.

Businesses such as law firms, financial institutions, or doctors' offices should not be using free services; yet surprisingly there is a lot of this activity. These free services are not breaking privacy laws. The problem is these services are lacking governance which creates gaps or other exploitable opportunities primarily because they are unsanctioned and unmanaged. There is no chain of custody and there is not yet a way to effectively document who has manipulated the data. Services like Dropbox, Yahoo and Google are perfectly safe, however they do not meet standards such as The Health Insurance Portability and Accountability Act of 1996 (HIPAA).

While GoDaddy is probably the more well-known name, for my webhosting solution I use Verio. Like many of the other service providers, Verio is involved with hardware and software. Verio also reserves domains. This is where I rent and maintain my domain names.

There are many free cloud Email services such as Google, Yahoo and Microsoft, but today most businesses are looking for a personalized domain and Email. Duncan's cloud architects have tinkered with dozens of Email providers and have decided that the best cloud-based Email system available is Microsoft Exchange. Microsoft Exchange works exceptionally well with all smart phones, tablets, on the Web or, as with most of us using Microsoft Outlook, on our desktop. Exchange used in concert with Outlook is an excellent productivity solution. Business-focused tools give you options to sync and share your calendar or delegate access and folder permissions. For greater collaboration and accountability, you can integrate Microsoft's SharePoint. SharePoint is likened to current organizational intranets. While currently undervalued, SharePoint is gaining new traction with the practical functionality offered in SharePoint 2013. It is also gaining more acceptance because PaaS and IaaS providers have begun to embrace and bundle this software as a service (SaaS) offering.

Cloud commerce is all about money transfers and there are many online providers. My choice is PayPal. PayPal is reliable and simple to use and with PayPal I have no worries about theft or scams because PayPal has a history of accountability and is subject to the US economic sanction list and interventions required by US laws. However, PayPal has horrible documented customer service and this is where a lot of frustration can occur. Hence, they are an example of where a cloud services brokerage can be your middleman.

For my bookkeeping and accounts receivable I use a cloud services provider called FreshBooks. Freshbooks is a great application. I accept payments with credit cards, PayPal, and twelve other payment options. It allows me to import expenses from my bank account, credit cards, and snap photos of my receipts. I can even attach an expense to an invoice and re-bill that invoice. Freshbooks, as an example of SaaS, saves me time and money. The financial system a company chooses to use is a big deal. Before Freshbooks I used Peachtree Accounting software for several years but grew tired of annual fees and costly planned upgrades that seemed frivolous. I have used other related SaaS and also recommend Quickbooks Online, however for my purpose FreshBooks suits me best for its simplicity.

In concert with my accounting system I use HighRise accompanied by RightSignature for customer relationship management. According to EnterpriseAppsToday.com, February 2013, Salesforce.com is the most popular customer relationship management (CRM) sales application. I looked at using this, however I felt it locked me into too much of a controlled environment, it was too expensive, and the end user license agreement (EULA) was problematic.

All of us know the inconvenience of running documents between parties to have them signed and archived. In conjunction with in-house processing, RightSignature has made tracking signatures and executed documents systematic. I send my prospect-turned-client a EULA and they easily sign it online with their mouse or their fingernail on their device of choice. I have had multiple documents returned electronically in the time it took to send, read, sign and return a single piece of paper.

Productivity tools and solutions are all for naught without connectivity. The cloud evaporates without consistent bandwidth available within a redundant telecommunications infrastructure.

Most of us cannot afford the benefits and speed of a private fiber-optic highway. It is out there, though, through companies like US Signal out of Grand Rapids, Michigan. US Signal has over 14,000 network miles that run in and out of its virtual data centers from Minneapolis, St. Paul to Pittsburgh and points north and south.

Like similar entities throughout the world, US Signal rents its infrastructure to public carriers such as AT&T, Sprint, Verizon, and numerous regional telecoms. Unfortunately, when it comes right down to it, most of us are limited by a single point of failure due to carrier access within the "last mile." Meaning, often there is only one carrier who has access to our office building, city block or rural location. This reality can be troublesome yet overcome with the help of a CSB. A CSB can assist with facilitating a second or even third access option such as cable, public Wi-Fi or cell tethering for office-based workers. A CSB can also be of assistance when signals go down.

AT&T provides me closed-loop access for DSL and I use a Voice over Internet Protocol (VoIP) provider for my phone system. I use Fonality for its longevity in the marketplace. While seemingly still in its infancy, VoIP allows me to host conference calls for both internal and external attendants with complete moderator control. There is a "Heads up Display" feature that makes it easy to connect with my team using built-in instant messaging and I can easily add and remove users.

There you have it, my public cloud ecosystem addressing core communication and collaboration needs as well as resources such as Email. You can probably estimate the amount of research and time it took to select which cloud services providers to utilize. I can speak to these providers as an end-user and as a broker who offers productivity bundles to consumers like you.

With the cloud's foundation, my IT ecosystem is no longer like spaghetti. It is now streamlined and simpler to manage. With the reduction of servers, software, and maintenance, I now spend more time concentrating on my business.

Points of Interest:

1. Utility computing is the resourcing of computing services (computation, storage, and services) as a metered service.
2. While using free services such as Google and Yahoo are safe options, you are relinquishing data control which may be used for advertising and commoditization.
3. Moving Email to the cloud is one of the most beneficial things a business can experience.
4. There are several PaaS and IaaS providers equal in services.
5. The cloud can help streamline and simplify your IT configuration.

J.F.D Landscapes, Inc.

Joe loved sifting through the mail at the end of the day. It relaxed him. It was the first time in his 16-hour day that he could sit down, other than when he was in his truck. He leaned back in his office chair, kicking off his boots while lifting his feet onto his desk and opening envelopes. It felt really good to be out of the hot sun and off the job sites. But Joe's day wasn't finished, he had to review each employee's timesheet and all the unique customer logs which had been input throughout the day in his industry-specific Customer Resource Management (CRM) software known as Timescapes. Additionally, it was time to forward billing and paycheck information to his bookkeeper in Florida.

Joe is the owner of J.F.D. Landscapes, Inc., a full-service company located close to Cleveland, Ohio just a few miles from the quaint village of Chagrin Falls. Joe opened his company in 1989. He started out as a kid with a truck, a lawnmower, some basic landscaping tools, and a friend to help him. Twenty plus years later he has a million dollar business with twenty-six employees, three supervisors, one full-time office person, and the aforementioned part-time bookkeeper in Florida.

As Joe sorted through the pile of bills, payments, and junk mail, a sky blue flyer caught his eye:

JOIN US IN THE CLOUD. BASIC CLOUD BUNDLE: IT INFRASTRUCTURE THAT'S ECONOMICAL, SCALABLE, AND SECURE, ONLY $249.95. CONTACT THIS SPECIALIST CLOUD SERVICES BROKERAGE FOR A FREE CONSULTATION.

Interesting, Joe thought. He had been considering moving to the cloud for a while. Joe loved technology and all of the applications on his iPhone. Recently, he had been reading a lot about the benefits of running a business in the cloud. Unfortunately, he was by no means knowledgeable enough to make the move on his own which was the reason his IT infrastructure had become stagnant. A specialist cloud services brokerage (SCSB) could be exactly what he had needed.

Joe currently had one on-site server that hosted and stored his Email, QuickBooks, Timescapes, and data. Joe and his team used a virtual private network (VPN) to provide remote access to the office server from home. Most companies use a VPN to access their office computers.

Joe had been using a local IT guy. He thought his name was Ryan. Or it could be Brian. He couldn't remember. He had gone through so many IT guys over the years that he didn't find a reason to remember their names. Joe knew this was not the best way to run his small business and came to the realization that a transition to the cloud might be beneficial. But that didn't matter much right now - it was summer - smack dab in the middle of his busy season. The cloud would have to wait until winter. Joe took the SCSB's flyer and tucked it safely in his manila IT folder for winter.

The temperature cooled, the leaves were cleaned up just in time for a cozy blanket of snow, and Joe's business went from booming to boring. Joe could finally get to work spiffing up his back office and addressing those pesky tasks that didn't get his full attention during the busy season. His first order of business was addressing his IT infrastructure.

Joe pulled the flyer from the SCSB out of his files. He wondered if the special pricing would still be valid six months later. He wouldn't know until he called, no time like the present. Joe picked up the phone and dialed.

The sales person who answered the phone at the SCSB was friendly and helpful. She explained to Joe that there was not a one-size fits all service and that they needed to send out an evaluation form to help the cloud architect better assist them. The sales person got Joe's Email address and sent over a survey that would help the SCSB in figuring out the needs of Joe's business. These questions would help to streamline the process and allow the SCSB to do a deep dive into his core IT needs, some needs that his company may not even know it has. The sales person set up an appointment for Joe to meet Don who would be Joe's cloud architect. Don would do an evaluation and if hired, would shadow Joe's project through to completion. Don would also evaluate Joe's business processes and inform him of offerings that were best suited to his needs and budget.

Don went out to see Joe shortly after the SCSB received the questionnaire. Don was an atypical techie in his early 40's. He had been in the "race to the bottom" for almost 20 years and had his hands in almost every area of computing at one point or another. It took this type of business-savvy IT person to appreciate the cloud. Don said it took the right IT guy to champion the cloud.

Don drove for what felt like hours from downtown Cleveland to the far eastside suburbs to get to Joe's office. He passed several horse farms and even a few cows along the way. He gathered his computer bag, put on his gloves and pulled his hat over his head for his walk into the small office trailer. A bell jingled as he pushed his way through the doorway. Joe met Don just inside the door and began talking immediately.

Once Don understood Joe's configuration, he began his evaluation of the last mile. How was Joe connected to the world? For Don, and others like him, this is an important undertaking and the first thing that a SCSB should do before making any suggestions. There is no need to begin if the situation or environment does not allow for bandwidth and connectivity redundancy. Joe's provider was Time Warner Cable and the bandwidth was sufficient to begin building his cloud ecosystem.

Don came back in from checking the lines. He kicked the snow off his boots and sat down with Joe at his desk. Don laid out solutions based on the research that his support team had conducted. He carefully went over each cloud-based solution that his team had come up with to replace the server based software that Joe was running at the time. "There is a cloud-based solution for the QuickBooks software you are running now. This is a fabulous solution to help you work better with your employee in Florida." Don explained that it would be easy to migrate this to the cloud because Joe was already using the on-site version of QuickBooks. Don also explained all of the benefits of the cloud version of QuickBooks: easy access for his accountant, a mobile application, the ability to send invoices, scan receipts, accept credit cards, and the ability to plug into well over 100 small business apps. Don explained that although there were several cloud-based accounting options available, from a retraining perspective it was always best, if practicable, to go with what you know. Joe was sold on this approach.

Don went on to explain an Email option that would replace his on-site system using Microsoft Exchange provided through Rackspace. Don explained how there would be a small monthly fee per person as opposed to the traditional capital expenditure and related maintenance. Although there are several cloud-based Email options, including free services such as Gmail for business, it would be best for Joe to migrate over to Microsoft Exchange as he was already using the on-site server based Microsoft Exchange program. Also, given answers on Joe's survey, Gmail was not the best option because Google commoditizes user data.

"What options do you have to replace Timescapes?" Joe asked.

"Unfortunately, there is no public cloud solution to replace your Timescapes software," Don replied.

"Well, that is unfortunate. I was hoping that both my supervisors and I would be able to access the software from the job sites rather than physically having to deliver the day's paperwork to the office. Also, I wanted to start spending part of the winters in Florida and if this isn't accessible I won't be able to do that," Joe said, tapping his pen.

Don placed his laptop on Joe's desk. "Let me show you this option," he said as he pulled out his iPad and turned it on.

Joe waited to see what Don had in store. Don turned the iPad around to show Joe.

There it was, a classic Microsoft desktop…on his iPad. "Now that is cool!" Joe said with an approving nod.

"This is a desktop service that we offer. This would give you access to TimeScape from anywhere in the world."

Joe started chewing on his pen, just like he always did when he was thinking. "Is this a private cloud?"

"Good question. It is not. In your case it would be a hybrid cloud. We would be optimizing your local server for the sole use of Timescapes because at this time there is no SaaS solution. All of your other systems would be running on the public cloud environment," Don explained.

Don continued to discuss the benefits of a SCSB that included unified billing and unified management. If Joe ever decided that a service provider was not working out he could cancel at any time without a penalty or termination fee because Joe was shielded by the brokerage. Don told Joe that he would come and set up all of the options that they had discussed. He would migrate all of the data and set up all of the mailboxes and access points.

Joe was happy with what Don had come up with. Almost his entire business would be run on the public cloud. Joe was grateful that he wouldn't be burdened with coordinating his set-up or managing the individual cloud services providers. Not only was the solution completely turn-key, he had hired a trusted team to watch his back.

On December 17, 2011, Joe began his move to the cloud. The data migration took a total of two weeks. He was surprised at how well the whole project was organized and implemented. He was even more surprised that it took only 24-hours to "flip the switch" from on-site to the cloud once the migration was complete.

Joe and his team are now able to work seamlessly, everywhere. Productivity is up and he is saving money.

Thanks to the cloud Joe started spending his winters in the sun.

Points of Interest:

1. A SCSB can assess your IT infrastructure and recommend productivity solutions to build your cloud IT ecosystem.
2. There are not always immediate options for niche industry specific software, however that does not mean there isn't a solution.
3. There are many applications, known as SaaS, which are intended to save you time and simplify your workflow.
4. You can assist your SCSB in coming up with your cloud IT ecosystem by answering a simple questionnaire.
5. Cloud-based services allow you to run your business from anywhere.

Alan Black Enterprises, Inc.

Tony Jones was running final reports when a voice came over the intercom, "Tony Jones, line one. Tony Jones, line one." As IT Manager at Acme Co., Tony was accustomed to last-minute calls when he was trying to end his day. Something was always breaking, someone was always having trouble, a computer was always freezing. Most companies don't realize it, but IT is the backbone of their existence.

"This is Tony," he said holding the phone with his chin as he was facilitating the final reports for the day. "Hello, Tony. This is Cliff Henderson. I am a recruiter from IT Recruiters in Dayton, Ohio. How are you today?"

"Good," Tony said hesitantly. Tony hadn't reached out to any recruitment companies, but he certainly knew the high demand for good IT professionals. Recruiters would do almost anything to find their clients high quality employees. He was in shock that someone actually came to the opposite side of the state to find him.

"I am calling about a client here in Dayton. They are looking for someone to fill the position of Director of Information and Technology Systems. They are looking for someone with innovative ideas in regards to IT." Cliff quietly waited for a response but got nothing.

Tony was very curious who the company could possibly be. The position could be a great opportunity – if the job was with the right organization.

"Are you there?" Cliff asked.

"I am. Can you give me some information about the employer?"

"I'd love to. Would you be able to put aside a few minutes for us to meet and discuss the opportunity further, Mr. Jones?" And so it began.

Tony found out that the company was Alan Black Enterprises, one of Acme's competitors. Founded in 1981 by a former professional athlete, ABE has over 600 employees, an excess of $500 million dollars in annual sales, and core competencies across several industries including Automotive, Medical, Life Sciences, Energy, and Industrial. Tony couldn't pass up the opportunity to run the IT department for such a large company. He took the job at ABE a month later, opting to work for Acme Co. for a couple more weeks prior to giving his two weeks notice so he could prepare for his move to Dayton.

Luckily for Acme, Tony is an honest employee and he had no intentions of stealing any of Acme's customer information or any other proprietary data that lives on their servers. However, if Acme had a SCSB in place and there was data slippage they would have been alerted because a SCSB would be monitoring the daily data activities of each employee. If anything suspicious or out-of-the-norm had occurred, the SCSB would notify a specified list of company executives.

ABE was a change from Tony's last position where everything was centered on the automotive industry. What both companies had in common was that they had a lot of inventory to monitor, items to ship, employees to manage, and money to move around. It was Tony's job to ensure that the IT applications managing each of those things were under control and up and running at all times.

On Tony's first day he met with his new boss, Albert Farnham. Albert was a jovial man. He gave Tony the grand tour of the offices and explained the set up. Typical of most offices, ABE had its servers hidden out of the way. A lot of the servers were over 8-years old. They were in dire need of replacement. Tony's heart sank when he saw the hardware for the first time. This wasn't what he expected.

He wasn't planning to have to start off by telling his new bosses that they would need to dish out at least $100,000 in hardware and licenses.

Tony sat across from Albert, twiddling his thumbs nervously, ready to give him the bad news. Albert sipped his coffee and went through a stack of notes on his desk. Tony couldn't bring himself to look up as he was delivering the news, "I took a look at your system and…"

"It is in awful condition, I know. Whole thing needs ripping out…." Albert interrupted.

"Yes, it does," Tony said sitting up.

Over the next several weeks, Tony took an extensive look at ABE's IT infrastructure and how each sub-system interacted. Each branch of the company was running different servers and phone systems, even different versions of the same enterprise resource planning software (ERP) system. The previous Director of Information and Technology Systems had started the process of switching the company over to Microsoft 365 several months prior to Tony taking over the position. Tony was relieved that the previous director had made this move. This eliminated the need for patches and upgrades at every location. Microsoft SharePoint was added with Microsoft 365. This common portal for all employees would allow for greater collaboration and coordination. Albert told Tony that it had only taken a weekend at each location to transfer anywhere from 35-50 employees from their on-site Microsoft Exchange servers to Microsoft 365. There were a few requirements to address on each user's Outlook but it was a seamless transfer. The employees seemed to not notice the difference.

Other than the implementation of the cloud Email system, the company's IT needed a complete overhaul. Tony decided to take on the huge task of putting every location on the same system so that every location's data would be accessible seamlessly. Figuring out how to best do that was the bigger challenge. Tony knew the usual options, all of the traditional IT solutions, however Tony wanted to take ABE in a different direction - Tony wanted to take all of ABE to the cloud.

While working at Acme, Inc., Tony had implemented a cloud-based ERP system called Plex designed specifically for the manufacturing industry. He had spent months researching Plex prior to implementation. At the time, he was unsure how an ERP system would work in the cloud and if it would be able to handle the massive amount of processing. The more he spoke with others about the service, the more secure he felt with adding it into Acme's IT ecosystem. Plex turned out to be a very successful addition to the IT infrastructure at Acme. Tony knew that implementing Plex at ABE would eliminate the need to purchase and maintain on-site servers and the licensing to go along with them, thus creating a uniform system across all of ABE's locations. Moreover, the use of cloud-based applications would also lighten the load on his tiny IT Department. ABE had five full-time IT people to run all the facilities in the United States and Canada.

For their phone system, Tony had decided to use Voice over Internet Protocol (VoIP) provided by Alteva, a BroadSoft solution. He was very excited about this phone system. This was a very new and innovative product. Although the chances were slim that the Internet would go down, this system provided failover to a backup phone line.

Tony had created a plan that was prepared for current and future users, thus he believed he could justify the cloud for all of their business requirements based on a pay-as-you-go monthly subscription that he was sure his new boss would embrace.

Tony tried to pretend he wasn't nervous as he knocked on Albert's door.

"Come in," the jovial voice yelled out.

"I've completed my cloud strategy," Tony said trying to cover up the frog in his throat.

"Wonderful," Albert said reaching across the table for the proposal, "have a seat."

Tony was hesitant. He didn't want Albert reviewing it in front of him. That would only make him more uncomfortable. But it seemed he didn't have a choice. Albert began to read while sipping his coffee. All Tony could do was look around the room and wait…and wait…and wait.

Finally, "This is fabulous!"

"Are you okay with all of the cloud solutions?" Tony asked.

"I am. I need to get confirmation but once I do I think this is a perfect plan. Just one question." *This is it. The question that will kill the deal…* "When can we start the process?"

Tony grinned. He began implementing the project a month later.

Once the plan was in place it only took a few days to implement the Alteva phone systems at each location. The system is so simple it took less than an hour to teach even the most reluctant employees how to use it.

The Plex system was not as simple a rollover. This was not due to being in the cloud, but rather the nature of an ERP system. Each facility took 6-12 months to transfer over. The Plex Manufacturing Cloud was built specifically for the manufacturing industry. Plex works by putting the plant floor first, no matter what the plant is manufacturing – be it medication or automobiles. It then allows for all the necessary communications between the manufacturers and their customers and suppliers. Depending on the job requirements of the employees, the training took from a few hours to several weeks. Plex is a much simpler, more streamlined ERP than ABE had before.

Tony knew that not everyone would like these changes. He set out to make things go as smoothly as possible by educating all of the plant managers and creating simple, yet detailed documentation for each new tool. It didn't take long for all of the employees to embrace the cloud.

Tony is proud of his cloud-based IT ecosystem but he knows there are always ways to improve and grow. In April 2014, Tony decided to integrate SalesForce.com with ABE's Plex ERP system. ABE will have integration capabilities between customer data, demand, revenue forecasts and more that would sync between SalesForce.com, their CRM Solution, and their hosted ERP Solution, Plex Online. This reduces redundant data entry and data entry errors in general, and provides quick access to more real-time information from any connected device.

Points of Interest

1. A SCSB can be a watchdog for any suspicious employee behavior as it relates to accessing company data.
2. Companies with good leadership recognize the value of staying current with information technologies.
3. Legacy systems or old technology can be inefficient, expensive to maintain, and counterproductive to business goal achievement.
4. Companies that do not remain current with technology risk losing good people and their position in their marketplace.
5. With proper planning and education employee retraining can be kept to a minimum.

Cleveland State University

As Chief Information Officer of Cleveland State University, Bill Wilson oversees the IT services for over 17,000 students and 4,500 faculty and staff members. This is no small task. On a daily basis, Bill is faced with more moving pieces than one could possibly imagine, often including elements that have nothing to do with the actual technology.

This morning he is dealing with the human element, Iris Baxter, a secretary on the third floor of Rhodes Tower, which happened to be the same building in which his office was located. Funny, Bill thought he had heard screaming and fussing from below just before Iris burst into his office.

"I am not sure what you think you are doing, Mr. Wilson, but the office staff is not going to have it! No sir, we aren't! Are you going to be losing your printer, too? Are you? Are you?" she asked, waving her finger at the printer on Bill's desk.

Bill was a patient man. He waited for Iris to continue venting. He understood change was hard, especially when it came to technology, but was it really necessary for her to yell at him?

"Mrs. Baxter, I understand your concern. However, these new printers will be faster, use less ink, less paper, and less energy. They are easy to use and are centrally located between groups of office staff."

Bill had found a way, with the help of Xerox, to take the University from 2,100 printers down to just 300 printers. The savings was huge! "And just think how much more room you will have on your desk!" Bill added with a smile. He hoped Iris understood the need for change and the benefits that came along with it.

"I know I don't have a choice in this matter Mr. Wilson, but I am going to tell you that I don't have to like it. None of us do!" Iris did an about-face and marched out of his office.

The thing about technology that amazed Bill was when employees started out their careers with the technology implemented a certain way they were fine, but if you changed it, their world fell apart. And it wasn't that it just fell apart, they actually got mad at the company for doing something better for the organization.

Cleveland State University (CSU) is located in downtown Cleveland, Ohio. The school opened its doors in 1964; fifty years later CSU has more than 100,000 students and alumni. Cleveland State offers many disciplines and research facilities with 70 academic majors, 27 master's degree programs, two post-master's degrees, six doctoral degrees, and two law degrees through Cleveland Marshall Law School. According to the National Science Foundation, Cleveland State ranks among the top 20% of universities in research and development.

Bill couldn't be more proud about running the IT for this institution. As the C.I.O. for Cleveland State University, he oversees the Information Services and Technology Department (IS&T) that is responsible for student, faculty, and administrative computing, telecommunications, systems management, operations, and end-user services. He is responsible for the development of planning processes and management procedures to provide for the effective use of information technology across the institution, coordinating and ensuring steady progress on large-scale information technology projects. He provides oversight of the formulation and implementation of the University's technology strategic plan and its policies.

Bill knows that bad decisions would not only disrupt the productivity of the employees who worked at the school, but also impact the students who trusted the institution to educate them and to make good decisions that would enrich their lives.

But Bill also has a budget to work within. That is something he always has to consider. Technology in business is a constant juggling act.

For many years CSU was running on Lotus Notes for all Email. After months of research Bill decided it was time to switch from Cleveland State's on-site hosting Email servers to the cloud. This was going to be one of their largest and most visible projects. The server costs alone were $250,000 per year; it required dozens of servers to host just Email. The licensing fee was $80,000 per year. All of this seemed very inefficient to Bill.

At the end of 2012, CSU transferred its Email system over to Microsoft 365. Student Email accounts were transferred first. With over 70% of all students forwarding their Emails to another account anyway, the school decided to set up new Email addresses for the students, eliminating the need for a full data migration. The students were fully accepting of the new Email system. They didn't miss a beat. All Bill could do was hope that the faculty and staff responded as well as the students. Bill was aware that Email was a far more personal thing to older generations, who as a group tend to resist accepting new technology. He was unsure how far his hope would take him.

The migration of the 4,500 faculty and staff Emails, calendars, and contact lists took place over the summer; it took 45 days to complete the data migration. During that time there were only 200 help desk tickets issued from users, indicating a successful migration.

Bill was thrilled! The benefits of moving CSU's Email to Microsoft 365 in the cloud were huge. He had successfully unburdened the University of a substantial annual expense while expanding services. CSU no longer had to be responsible for related disaster recovery - Microsoft did. This was a huge relief for Bill and the institution. And since Microsoft recently agreed to keep all of their data in the United States, Bill was as comfortable as he could be with anything else out there.

While this may have been Bill's largest and most successful move to the cloud for CSU, it was not his first. His first move to the cloud was with Blackboard, CSU's online learning management system. Blackboard was the largest and most resource draining software that CSU had to host. It required a massive number of servers and back-ups. Four years ago, with the help of the e-Learning department, Bill moved the massive amounts of information from CSU's servers to Blackboard's servers. Blackboard charges them $120,000.00 a year to host their infrastructure in the cloud, but this is a fraction of what it was costing them to host it on-site. Besides the cost, Bill no longer has to worry about his servers going down, replacing the servers it took to host Blackboard every three years, or the disaster recovery issues that could never be fully remedied. Besides the benefit to the university, Bill also brought an upside to himself and his employees — fewer phone calls from faculty and staff when servers were on the fritz. A true win-win situation.

Bill was pleased with how things were going with the two largest software solutions running on the cloud. He had reduced costs and simplified how things ran.

But there were also more cloud solutions that Bill set up for CSU on the cloud.

Acalog, CSU's academic catalog management system, helps the university revise and publish curriculum. It enables publishing the catalog to several different mediums including print with a click of a button. This is the backbone of how students select their courses.

Kronos Time Management System assists in the tasks of monitoring employee time and attendance. It offers a simplified time and tracking software. Their software helped the HR department cut back on labor costs, minimize compliance risks, and improve workforce productivity. Bill was pleased that he was able to identify and implement technology that aided in solving such a huge problem facing the institution.

Bill was able to implement a cloud-based solution to solve a scheduling dilemma in the Guidance Department. The solution came from a company called Starfish Retention Services via their service, Starfish Connect. Through Starfish, the university encourages success by connecting students with the people and the resources they need to get ahead, facilitating meaningful contact among students, advisors, and instructors.

These software solutions were things the University didn't want to mess with or have to worry about backing up, and they all turned out to be cost effective, reliable solutions that simplified CSU's IT ecosystem.

Bill loves the results that the cloud brought him. He is currently looking at switching his PeopleSoft program, their Human Resource Management Systems (HRMS), and Customer Relationship Management (CRM) Software, over to WorkDay a cloud-based CRM and HRMS tool. Currently, CSU is paying between $800,000-$900,000 per year to run PeopleSoft. This cost includes servers and the staff it takes to oversee the software. By switching to WorkDay, Bill could eliminate the servers, the worry, and in some cases the need for staff. Bill had already decided that he wouldn't eliminate the staff but rather re-deploy them elsewhere. This would be his next move to the cloud and he was about ready for takeoff.

Bill was confident he was making the right decisions for CSU. He had often been asked about the safety of the data and wrestled with this early on but came to the realization that nothing is 100% safe. Besides, how could he protect the data better than Microsoft or Amazon? It just wasn't possible. Bill knew that the safest place for the university's material was in the cloud. Bill does not consider himself or the university to be particularly innovative with regards to their embrace of the cloud. Nonetheless, he is very proud of what they have achieved thus far.

Points of Interest:

1. The cloud can help with decreasing your overall hardware requirements, not just servers and processors, but ancillary equipment such as printers.
2. Transferring Email to the cloud can be a straightforward process.
3. Many large software companies offer cloud-based hosting solutions that provide disaster recovery options.
4. Implemented correctly, new technology does not have to be the "enemy" of a company's existing employees; that is, proper inclusion and education can overcome resistance to change.
5. There is a SaaS for just about anything.

Next Steps

Assess Your Current IT Infrastructure: Prepare for the Future

Whether you are personally handling your organization's transition to the cloud or overseeing it, the questions below will be helpful as you plan your way. The categories and questions are intended as a guide to the future of your IT. Answers to these questions will help you figure out what you need now as well as in the years to come. They will also help a broker understand your requirements.

Business Overview and Future Plans:

1. What do you see as the IT main service your company currently provides?
2. What are the computer programs (by name) that are most critical to your daily operation and what are their respective business functions?
3. Do you foresee adding any new business services or programs?
4. Would it be beneficial to be connected to another site?
5. How many employees use computers?
6. What type of work do you do with your computers?
7. Are there any current manual functions you would like to have automated?
8. Do you foresee any change in the number of people that use PC's in your organization over the next few months?
9. How old are your workstations, laptops, and servers?
10. Do you think you will need to add any servers?
11. How does your company use the Internet?
12. What is your company website address?
13. Do you have policies that govern employee use of Internet and electronic devices?

14. Do you have remote access to your network or Email?
15. Do you see your reliance on the Internet changing in the future?
16. What are your top priorities to address with IT?
17. If you could improve one thing about your IT situation, what would it be?
18. Do you use Voice over Internet Protocol (VoIP)? If yes, who is your provider?
19. What type of bandwidth aggregator / load balancer, if any, do you have in place?
20. Do you experience any virus / malware / spyware issues?
21. How do you back up your data: tape, disk, the cloud? And how often?
22. Are any of your systems virtualized?
23. Do you have a disaster recovery plan? If yes, what is your disaster recovery plan?

Email:

1. Where is your Email system located?
2. Approximately how many Email addresses/mailboxes do you need? (Usually it is one mailbox per user but sometimes there are special resource mailboxes.)
3. On which domains do you receive Email?
4. If you use Outlook for Email, do you use .pst files for storing Email messages?
5. Do you currently have spam filtering? If so, who is your provider?
6. Are you running any type of "special" system such as file transfer protocol (FTP) for sharing files with outside entities?
7. Do you use public folders in Outlook?
8. Do you have an existing Email server in place?
9. Do you have content filtering in place?
10. Do you have spam filtering in place?

Hardware:

1. What are the various makes and models of your workstations, laptops and servers?
2. How many servers do you have and what operating systems are they running?
3. How many laptops do you have and what operating systems are they running?
4. How many printers and scanners do you have and what makes and models?
5. How many workstations do you have and what operating systems are they running?
6. What version of Microsoft Office and Outlook are you currently running?
7. What version of Windows do you run? (e.g. XP, Vista, 7, 8)
8. Do you run any Macs?
9. Do your users have mobile devices? (e.g. Blackberries, iPhones, Androids) How many approximately?
10. Are you having any disk space issues on your servers?

IT Network(s):

1. What AntiVirus do you use for your network?
2. Do you have a diagram of your network?
3. Are there any known issues with your network at this time?
4. What is the type of back up software, hardware, strategy you use?
5. What type of Internet connection do you have and what are the speeds?
6. Do you receive notifications of back up success and failure?
7. Have you ever tested your backups and performed a successful restore?
8. Do you use Group Policies to lock down and control settings in your environment?
9. How many network drive letters do you currently have or would like to have?

10. Is your office connected to any other sites?

11. If your office is connected to other sites, how are they connected to each other?

12. What type of bandwidth aggregator or load balancer, if any, do you have in place?

IT and Telecommunications Staff In-house or otherwise:

1. Who takes care of your computers for you? Are they internal staff or third party?

2. If engaged with a service provider, are you currently in a contract?

3. Do you have server, desktop or network device monitoring in place?

4. Who is your Internet Service Provider (ISP)?

5. Do you have access to your domain name login information?

Middleware:

1. Do you use any wireless access points?

2. What type of firewall and/or router do you have in place?

Software:

1. Do you use Microsoft Access and have any database files you would like in the cloud?

2. Are any of the programs you use custom written?

3. Are there any software programs you would like to use but can't for one reason or another?

4. Do you run SharePoint in your organization? If yes, what version and how do you utilize it?

5. Do you have license information for desktop and server applications and operating systems?

6. What other software programs are supported other than those deemed critical to your daily operation?

Create a Gateway Cloud

A world of rentable options and services awaits you in the cloud:
- Bundled Solutions
- Cloud-Scale Provisioning
- Customer Support
- Service Level Agreement (SLA) monitoring
- Unified Management
- Unified Billing

Solutions offered by cloud services providers and ancillary vendors are seemingly endless. They purport to solve almost any business need and they are changing by the day. The level of noise created by the rapid evolution of cloud services has created a marketplace that is often overwhelming and daunting to navigate. Each category has numerous choices, each with its own benefits and pitfalls.

Trusting the life of your business to a cloud services provider that you have not vetted is nerve-racking. However, as your cloud middleman, a SCSB can assist you with developing a cloud strategy and selecting solutions for your cloud ecosystem while balancing your needs against available resources. I understand each business's requirements are unique, yet all businesses have the same basic technology needs: remote access, Email, and shared file storage. That is why, with the help of my cloud architects, we are providing you this gateway cloud option along with an assessment for evaluating and mapping your current IT infrastructure plus a resource guide for defining and selecting a cloud services brokerage.

I decided to open source this basic bundle because everyone should have the opportunity to experience the communication and collaboration tools offered by the cloud. By the end of this process, you will have the skills to build a cloud ecosystem. Don't worry about breaking something, you aren't dealing with fine china; everything is fixable and there are people available to help you. My research team and I worked with several companies on the way to developing this gateway cloud. We chose the following providers for your gateway cloud because of their customer service and intuitive user interfaces.

The first service in our gateway cloud is remote access. Remote access is as simple as it sounds. It allows a user to remotely access their personal computer anywhere from a web browser. Incidentally, I named it a gateway cloud because you are using your personal computer.

There are several providers that we promote when it comes to remote access, yet for this purpose we are suggesting LogMeIn Pro. Using LogMeIn Pro and the device of your choice you will be able to login to your personal computer and have access to it no matter where you happen to be.

There are two elements to LogMeIn Pro. The first piece of LogMeIn Pro is an executable (.exe), as we have come to know it, that you download onto your personal computer. This executable must be downloaded so you can use the cloud portion of LogMeIn Pro. After you have opened the lines of communication with LogMeIn Pro, you are able to remote onto your personal computer from a web browser. The setup of this powerful tool is simple. Go to LogMeIn.com and click on the **BUY** button located directly across from the **Pro** graphic.

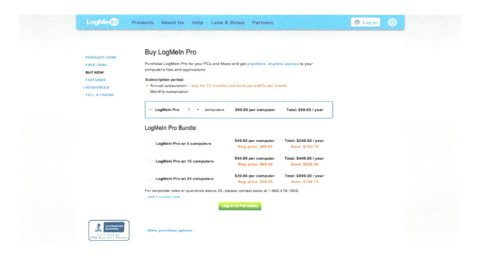

Simple as that! You will be with your personal computer even when you are without your personal computer. Keep in mind this is a gateway cloud, actually a baby hybrid that you can create on tenured equipment and operating systems. This is a hybrid cloud because you are going to utilize the public cloud and your on-site hardware, related middleware, and software. When you are ready to add to your cloud ecosystem or need help with your gateway cloud a SCSB is there to assist you.

The Email system we have chosen is Microsoft Exchange. Microsoft Exchange is a wonderful business productivity tool that offers Email, calendaring, tasks, contact management, and other functions and interfaces. It allows for rich collaboration including calendar and mailbox sharing. It also syncs with Outlook, Outlook Web App, and most popular mobile devices. It has a high level of spam filter capabilities to help with security.

We selected Rackspace as our cloud-based Microsoft Exchange provider. Rackspace makes the process of setting up Microsoft Exchange as easy as online shopping. The following images show you just how easy Rackspace is to set up a cloud-based Microsoft Exchange Server at Rackspace.com.

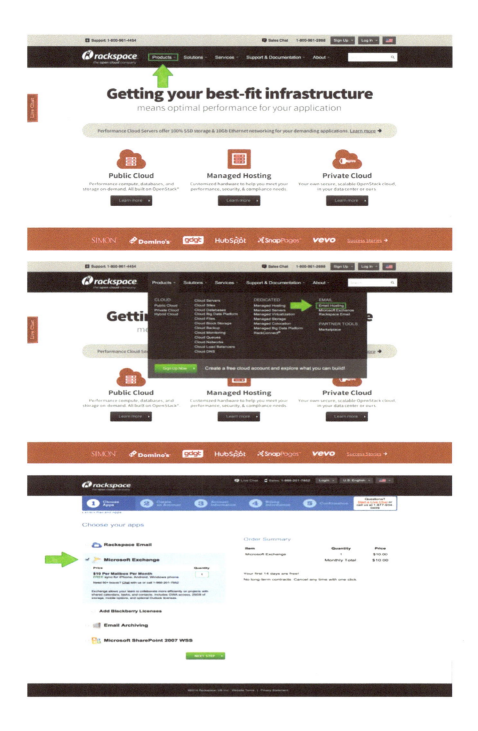

Once you set up the Microsoft Exchange services you will need to set up your Microsoft Outlook application.

To accompany the collaboration capabilities of Microsoft Exchange SharePoint, another Microsoft productivity tool, has been added to provide you with a company intranet and document management capabilities. SharePoint 2013 is feature-rich and also allows for security and versioning of file data. You remain in control of all of your documents so you continue to meet compliance requirements while accessing your documents from across devices. This software is also hosted on Rackspace and is just as easy to set up. Peek at the quantity boxes below. It is just like buying shoes from Zappos or this book from Amazon.

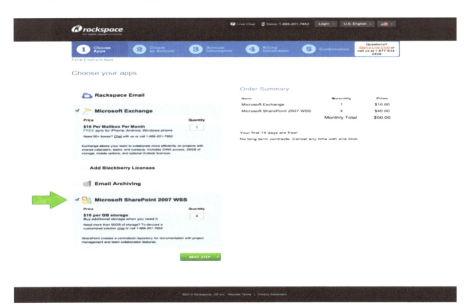

The last service in your gateway cloud is file storage and back up provided through Jungle Disk:

- Easily setup secure network drives for your users
- Robust online backup to protect your critical files
- Share files between multiple computers from anywhere
- Multi-way sync keeps files constantly up to date

• AES-256 encryption with a key you create and control

Across the office or around the globe, Jungle Disk allows fast, secure sharing and syncing of data between multiple users under one master account. It works just like a local letter drive (e.g. Computer (c:)).

Jungle Disk Workgroup Edition brings the power of the cloud to your business with secure backups, syncing capabilities, and data access. Powered by storage options from cloud leaders Rackspace and Amazon, Jungle Disk gives you everything your business needs in one easy to use package.

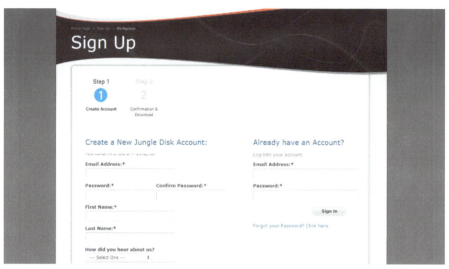

The price of file storage in the cloud is very reasonable and has no start-up costs. However, like most utilities this too is metered so it is important for you to understand your budget. After a few months of use you will begin to understand the amount of data you have and the amount of outgoing data you use each month.

There you have it - your gateway cloud. This obviously is just the beginning of what the cloud has to offer, but it is a good start and it covers the basics.

Points of Interest:

1. There are many cloud providers offering the same services. Some are more consumer friendly than others.
2. SCSB's should have more than one cloud provider per similar service.
3. There are basic cloud services that all businesses need.
4. A business can build on the basic "gateway cloud".
5. Everything is fixable when it comes to setting up your cloud ecosystem.

Select a Cloud Services Brokerage (CSB)

When looking for a CSB, assess their stance on risk management in general and ask candidates how they handle issues such software licensing, security, and management of service level agreements (SLA).

Know what you want from your Broker:
(For example)
- Governance
- Monitoring
- Provisioning

Know what type of brokerage you need or desire:
(For example)
- Simple cloud brokerage
- Full service brokerage
- Software as a Service brokerage
- Specialized cloud services brokerage

Remember a SCSB should be adding value such as: aggregation, arbitrage, or security, and where practicable, offering centralized command and control (governance and auditability) in addition to:
- Bundled Solutions
- Cloud-scale Provisioning
- Customer Support
- SLA Management
- Unified Billing
- Unified Management

When it comes to the public sector, in addition to their role as a middleman, the nature of the CSB is to stimulate the following:

- Maximized governmental purchasing power of cloud solutions across agencies or departments otherwise known as shared services
- Reduced duplication of cloud procurement
- Aggregated services reducing acquisition complexity
- Increased vendor competition and reduced pricing
- An ecosystem of partners – one location (e.g. marketplace or exchange) to find customized services
- The potential for value-added services such as federated security, service level agreement management, governance and policy management

"For both the public and private sectors a CSB can make it less expensive, easier, safer, and more productive for organizations to navigate, integrate, consume, and extend cloud services, particularly when they span multiple, diverse cloud services providers." – Gartner

Epilogue

After just a couple of decades of building and running our own in-house information technology (IT) infrastructures, we are slowly circling around to where we will do less maintenance and manipulation and much more consuming as a result of the utility called cloud computing.

From the ability to enjoy Netflix to treating healthcare patients around the world, we are increasingly able to focus more on the human element while more and more daily computing interactions occur M2M (machine to machine), IT resources will be more finite, secure and targeted. While this shift will eventually make our businesses more streamlined, the current impediment to wider acceptance of this utility is education and oversight of the soft side of technology.

Before we can make the proverbial jump to light speed, those of us in acquisition, leadership, and management roles must embrace the cloud's potential and then proactively manage the personalities, expectations, and abilities of our workforces. Without a doubt there will always be individuals who resist change. However, each generation becomes a little more adept at embracing the advances of technology than the one before it. Business will see a movement away from resistance to change as new generations move into the workforce and positions of management. Younger generations speak computing as a first language. This comprehension will alleviate the fear of technology and moreover the resistance to change. This is something that the business world has never seen before. This will allow for changes to be implemented more often, quickly and efficiently.

The migration to the cloud has now become inevitable. You should begin to investigate and move reasonable elements of your organization's IT demands to the cloud before you are forced to shift.

To support you in these endeavors there are cloud services brokerages. I predict that the CSB role will evolve to where they have the ultimate vantage point to monitor and manage of all of your cloud services. The CSB will be your IT trustee, helping you keep your business data safe and chaperoning purchases of your cloud services.

Acknowledgements

As with the inter-organizational cooperation and unique skills required to operate dynamic cloud services, producing a static product such as this book drew from similar relationships - there is no bibliography as perspectives are credited accordingly throughout this book.

I want to thank the following individuals for their talents:

Brad Burke
Brad Lipinski
Bob Coppedge
Clifford K. Henderson
Don Jones
Frank Kenny
Lindsay Preston
Ruthanne Myers-Fox
Sandy Barsky
Susan Rapp
Tiffany Bova

About the Author

Todd Lyle has become a leader in cloud computing with a focus on the human element. His fascination with the possibilities of information technology began when he was issued his first laptop computer while serving as a young officer in a U.S. Army aviation regiment in Korea. A bulky Zenith Supersport with only two functions was his first brush with "mobile" computing. After leaving active duty Lyle obtained a Master's Degree in Risk Management and accepted a position with Microsoft, where he became a group manager responsible for Consumer Support. It was while working at Microsoft that Lyle became interested in the myriad ways that information technology can improve overall business productivity.

Being well aware of the growing potential of cloud computing, in 2007 Lyle launched Duncan LLC to participate in this exciting new industry. At Duncan, Lyle assembled a business and technology savvy team that created ingenious cloud computing service bundles that focus on affordable and customer-centric solutions for the business world.

While running Duncan LLC, Lyle wrote of his enthusiasm for the potential of cloud computing. This attracted the attention of Gartner (NYSE: IT), an internationally recognized information technology research and advisory company. In April 2012 Gartner awarded Duncan LLC "Cool Vendor" status. Gartner defines a Cool Vendor as a company that offers technologies or solutions that are innovative, impactful, and intriguing. Encouraged by this recognition, Lyle decided to become a voice for the everyday business person and the result is this book. May it provide you with the information and motivation you need to benefit from the many possibilities that cloud computing can bring to your organization.

www.ingramcontent.com/pod-product-compliance
Lightning Source LLC
Chambersburg PA
CBHW041144050326
40689CB00001B/474